WINE TASTING
LOGBOOK

THIS BELONGS TO	
FIRST ENTRY DATE	LAST ENTRY DATE

NOTE: GLOSSARY OF TERMS CAN BE FOUND AT BACK OF BOOK

CONTENTS

WINE #	NAME	PRODUCER	DATE TASTED	PAGE #
1				4
2				6
3				8
4				10
5				12
6				14
7				16
8				18
9				20
10				22
11				24
12				26
13				28
14				30
15				32
16				34
17				36
18				38
19				40
20				42
21				44
22				46
23				48
24				50
25				52

CONTENTS

WINE #	NAME	PRODUCER	DATE TASTED	PAGE #
26				54
27				56
28				58
29				60
30				62
31				64
32				66
33				68
34				70
35				72
36				74
37				76
38				78
39				80
40				82
41				84
42				86
43				88
44				90
45				92
46				94
47				96
48				98
49				100
50				102

TASTING SHEET 01

WINE DETAILS

WINE NAME		DATE
PRODUCER		REGION / APPELLATION
VARIETAL		TYPE
VINTAGE	AGE	ALCOHOL %
PRICE	PURCHASED FROM	BOTTLE SIZE
NOTES		

VISUAL

CLARITY	BRIGHTNESS
INTENSITY	VISCOSITY
COLOR	SECONDARY COLOR
MENISCUS	OTHER / NOTES

PALATE / SMELL

CONDITION	INTENSITY
FRUIT	FLOWER / HERB / OTHER

TASTING SHEET 01

PALATE / SMELL (CONTINUED)

AROMA	EARTH
OAK	OTHER / NOTES

STRUCTURE / TASTE

SWEETNESS	BODY
ACIDITY	ALCOHOL
TANNIN	COMPLEXITY
LENGTH	BALANCE

NOTES

DISCUSSION

NOTES	SUGGESTED PAIRINGS

SCORECARD

OVERALL QUALITY

1	2	3	4	5	6	7	8	9	10

TASTE

1	2	3	4	5	6	7	8	9	10

VALUE FOR MONEY

1	2	3	4	5	6	7	8	9	10

TASTING SHEET 02

WINE DETAILS

WINE NAME	DATE
PRODUCER	REGION / APPELLATION
VARIETAL	TYPE

VINTAGE	AGE	ALCOHOL %
PRICE	PURCHASED FROM	BOTTLE SIZE

NOTES

VISUAL

CLARITY	BRIGHTNESS
INTENSITY	VISCOSITY
COLOR	SECONDARY COLOR
MENISCUS	OTHER / NOTES

PALATE / SMELL

CONDITION	INTENSITY
FRUIT	FLOWER / HERB / OTHER

TASTING SHEET 02

PALATE / SMELL (CONTINUED)

AROMA	EARTH
OAK	OTHER / NOTES

STRUCTURE / TASTE

SWEETNESS	BODY
ACIDITY	ALCOHOL
TANNIN	COMPLEXITY
LENGTH	BALANCE

NOTES

DISCUSSION

NOTES	SUGGESTED PAIRINGS

SCORECARD

OVERALL QUALITY

1	2	3	4	5	6	7	8	9	10

TASTE

1	2	3	4	5	6	7	8	9	10

VALUE FOR MONEY

1	2	3	4	5	6	7	8	9	10

TASTING SHEET 03

WINE DETAILS

WINE NAME	DATE

PRODUCER	REGION / APPELLATION

VARIETAL	TYPE

VINTAGE	AGE	ALCOHOL %

PRICE	PURCHASED FROM	BOTTLE SIZE

NOTES

VISUAL

CLARITY	BRIGHTNESS

INTENSITY	VISCOSITY

COLOR	SECONDARY COLOR

MENISCUS	OTHER / NOTES

PALATE / SMELL

CONDITION	INTENSITY

FRUIT	FLOWER / HERB / OTHER

TASTING SHEET 03

PALATE / SMELL (CONTINUED)

AROMA	EARTH
OAK	OTHER / NOTES

STRUCTURE / TASTE

SWEETNESS	BODY
ACIDITY	ALCOHOL
TANNIN	COMPLEXITY
LENGTH	BALANCE

NOTES

DISCUSSION

NOTES	SUGGESTED PAIRINGS

SCORECARD

OVERALL QUALITY

1	2	3	4	5	6	7	8	9	10

TASTE

1	2	3	4	5	6	7	8	9	10

VALUE FOR MONEY

1	2	3	4	5	6	7	8	9	10

TASTING SHEET 04

WINE DETAILS

WINE NAME		DATE	
PRODUCER		REGION / APPELLATION	
VARIETAL		TYPE	
VINTAGE	AGE	ALCOHOL %	
PRICE	PURCHASED FROM	BOTTLE SIZE	
NOTES			

VISUAL

CLARITY	BRIGHTNESS
INTENSITY	VISCOSITY
COLOR	SECONDARY COLOR
MENISCUS	OTHER / NOTES

PALATE / SMELL

CONDITION	INTENSITY
FRUIT	FLOWER / HERB / OTHER

TASTING SHEET 04

PALATE / SMELL (CONTINUED)

AROMA	EARTH
OAK	OTHER / NOTES

STRUCTURE / TASTE

SWEETNESS	BODY
ACIDITY	ALCOHOL
TANNIN	COMPLEXITY
LENGTH	BALANCE

NOTES

DISCUSSION

NOTES	SUGGESTED PAIRINGS

SCORECARD

OVERALL QUALITY

1	2	3	4	5	6	7	8	9	10

TASTE

1	2	3	4	5	6	7	8	9	10

VALUE FOR MONEY

1	2	3	4	5	6	7	8	9	10

TASTING SHEET 05

WINE DETAILS

WINE NAME		DATE	
PRODUCER		REGION / APPELLATION	
VARIETAL		TYPE	
VINTAGE	AGE		ALCOHOL %
PRICE	PURCHASED FROM		BOTTLE SIZE
NOTES			

VISUAL

CLARITY	BRIGHTNESS
INTENSITY	VISCOSITY
COLOR	SECONDARY COLOR
MENISCUS	OTHER / NOTES

PALATE / SMELL

CONDITION	INTENSITY
FRUIT	FLOWER / HERB / OTHER

TASTING SHEET 05

PALATE / SMELL (CONTINUED)

AROMA	EARTH
OAK	OTHER / NOTES

STRUCTURE / TASTE

SWEETNESS	BODY
ACIDITY	ALCOHOL
TANNIN	COMPLEXITY
LENGTH	BALANCE

NOTES

DISCUSSION

NOTES	SUGGESTED PAIRINGS

SCORECARD

OVERALL QUALITY

| 1 | 2 | 3 | 4 | 5 | 6 | 7 | 8 | 9 | 10 |

TASTE

| 1 | 2 | 3 | 4 | 5 | 6 | 7 | 8 | 9 | 10 |

VALUE FOR MONEY

| 1 | 2 | 3 | 4 | 5 | 6 | 7 | 8 | 9 | 10 |

TASTING SHEET 06

WINE DETAILS	
WINE NAME	DATE
PRODUCER	REGION / APPELLATION
VARIETAL	TYPE
VINTAGE	AGE	ALCOHOL %
PRICE	PURCHASED FROM	BOTTLE SIZE
NOTES	

VISUAL	
CLARITY	BRIGHTNESS
INTENSITY	VISCOSITY
COLOR	SECONDARY COLOR
MENISCUS	OTHER / NOTES

PALATE / SMELL	
CONDITION	INTENSITY
FRUIT	FLOWER / HERB / OTHER

TASTING SHEET 06

PALATE / SMELL (CONTINUED)	
AROMA	EARTH
OAK	OTHER / NOTES

STRUCTURE / TASTE	
SWEETNESS	BODY
ACIDITY	ALCOHOL
TANNIN	COMPLEXITY
LENGTH	BALANCE
NOTES	

DISCUSSION	
NOTES	SUGGESTED PAIRINGS

SCORECARD

OVERALL QUALITY

1	2	3	4	5	6	7	8	9	10

TASTE

1	2	3	4	5	6	7	8	9	10

VALUE FOR MONEY

1	2	3	4	5	6	7	8	9	10

TASTING SHEET 07

WINE DETAILS	
WINE NAME	DATE
PRODUCER	REGION / APPELLATION
VARIETAL	TYPE
VINTAGE	AGE	ALCOHOL %
PRICE	PURCHASED FROM	BOTTLE SIZE
NOTES	

VISUAL	
CLARITY	BRIGHTNESS
INTENSITY	VISCOSITY
COLOR	SECONDARY COLOR
MENISCUS	OTHER / NOTES

PALATE / SMELL	
CONDITION	INTENSITY
FRUIT	FLOWER / HERB / OTHER

TASTING SHEET 07

PALATE / SMELL (CONTINUED)

AROMA	EARTH
OAK	OTHER / NOTES

STRUCTURE / TASTE

SWEETNESS	BODY
ACIDITY	ALCOHOL
TANNIN	COMPLEXITY
LENGTH	BALANCE

NOTES

DISCUSSION

NOTES	SUGGESTED PAIRINGS

SCORECARD

OVERALL QUALITY
| 1 | 2 | 3 | 4 | 5 | 6 | 7 | 8 | 9 | 10 |

TASTE
| 1 | 2 | 3 | 4 | 5 | 6 | 7 | 8 | 9 | 10 |

VALUE FOR MONEY
| 1 | 2 | 3 | 4 | 5 | 6 | 7 | 8 | 9 | 10 |

TASTING SHEET 08

WINE DETAILS	
WINE NAME	DATE
PRODUCER	REGION / APPELLATION
VARIETAL	TYPE
VINTAGE / AGE	ALCOHOL %
PRICE / PURCHASED FROM	BOTTLE SIZE
NOTES	

VISUAL	
CLARITY	BRIGHTNESS
INTENSITY	VISCOSITY
COLOR	SECONDARY COLOR
MENISCUS	OTHER / NOTES

PALATE / SMELL	
CONDITION	INTENSITY
FRUIT	FLOWER / HERB / OTHER

TASTING SHEET 08

PALATE / SMELL (CONTINUED)

AROMA	EARTH
OAK	OTHER / NOTES

STRUCTURE / TASTE

SWEETNESS	BODY
ACIDITY	ALCOHOL
TANNIN	COMPLEXITY
LENGTH	BALANCE
NOTES	

DISCUSSION

NOTES	SUGGESTED PAIRINGS

SCORECARD

OVERALL QUALITY

| 1 | 2 | 3 | 4 | 5 | 6 | 7 | 8 | 9 | 10 |

TASTE

| 1 | 2 | 3 | 4 | 5 | 6 | 7 | 8 | 9 | 10 |

VALUE FOR MONEY

| 1 | 2 | 3 | 4 | 5 | 6 | 7 | 8 | 9 | 10 |

TASTING SHEET 09

WINE DETAILS

WINE NAME		DATE
PRODUCER		REGION / APPELLATION
VARIETAL		TYPE

VINTAGE	AGE	ALCOHOL %
PRICE	PURCHASED FROM	BOTTLE SIZE

NOTES

VISUAL

CLARITY	BRIGHTNESS
INTENSITY	VISCOSITY
COLOR	SECONDARY COLOR
MENISCUS	OTHER / NOTES

PALATE / SMELL

CONDITION	INTENSITY
FRUIT	FLOWER / HERB / OTHER

TASTING SHEET 09

PALATE / SMELL (CONTINUED)

AROMA	EARTH
OAK	OTHER / NOTES

STRUCTURE / TASTE

SWEETNESS	BODY
ACIDITY	ALCOHOL
TANNIN	COMPLEXITY
LENGTH	BALANCE

NOTES	

DISCUSSION

NOTES	SUGGESTED PAIRINGS

SCORECARD

OVERALL QUALITY
1	2	3	4	5	6	7	8	9	10

TASTE
1	2	3	4	5	6	7	8	9	10

VALUE FOR MONEY
1	2	3	4	5	6	7	8	9	10

TASTING SHEET 10

WINE DETAILS	
WINE NAME	DATE
PRODUCER	REGION / APPELLATION
VARIETAL	TYPE
VINTAGE	AGE	ALCOHOL %
PRICE	PURCHASED FROM	BOTTLE SIZE
NOTES	

VISUAL	
CLARITY	BRIGHTNESS
INTENSITY	VISCOSITY
COLOR	SECONDARY COLOR
MENISCUS	OTHER / NOTES

PALATE / SMELL	
CONDITION	INTENSITY
FRUIT	FLOWER / HERB / OTHER

TASTING SHEET 10

PALATE / SMELL (CONTINUED)

AROMA	EARTH
OAK	OTHER / NOTES

STRUCTURE / TASTE

SWEETNESS	BODY
ACIDITY	ALCOHOL
TANNIN	COMPLEXITY
LENGTH	BALANCE

NOTES

DISCUSSION

NOTES	SUGGESTED PAIRINGS

SCORECARD

OVERALL QUALITY

| 1 | 2 | 3 | 4 | 5 | 6 | 7 | 8 | 9 | 10 |

TASTE

| 1 | 2 | 3 | 4 | 5 | 6 | 7 | 8 | 9 | 10 |

VALUE FOR MONEY

| 1 | 2 | 3 | 4 | 5 | 6 | 7 | 8 | 9 | 10 |

TASTING SHEET 11

WINE DETAILS	
WINE NAME	DATE
PRODUCER	REGION / APPELLATION
VARIETAL	TYPE
VINTAGE	AGE	ALCOHOL %
PRICE	PURCHASED FROM	BOTTLE SIZE
NOTES	

VISUAL	
CLARITY	BRIGHTNESS
INTENSITY	VISCOSITY
COLOR	SECONDARY COLOR
MENISCUS	OTHER / NOTES

PALATE / SMELL	
CONDITION	INTENSITY
FRUIT	FLOWER / HERB / OTHER

TASTING SHEET 11

PALATE / SMELL (CONTINUED)

AROMA	EARTH
OAK	OTHER / NOTES

STRUCTURE / TASTE

SWEETNESS	BODY
ACIDITY	ALCOHOL
TANNIN	COMPLEXITY
LENGTH	BALANCE

NOTES

DISCUSSION

NOTES	SUGGESTED PAIRINGS

SCORECARD

OVERALL QUALITY

| 1 | 2 | 3 | 4 | 5 | 6 | 7 | 8 | 9 | 10 |

TASTE

| 1 | 2 | 3 | 4 | 5 | 6 | 7 | 8 | 9 | 10 |

VALUE FOR MONEY

| 1 | 2 | 3 | 4 | 5 | 6 | 7 | 8 | 9 | 10 |

TASTING SHEET 12

WINE DETAILS

WINE NAME		DATE

PRODUCER	REGION / APPELLATION

VARIETAL	TYPE

VINTAGE	AGE	ALCOHOL %

PRICE	PURCHASED FROM	BOTTLE SIZE

NOTES

VISUAL

CLARITY	BRIGHTNESS

INTENSITY	VISCOSITY

COLOR	SECONDARY COLOR

MENISCUS	OTHER / NOTES

PALATE / SMELL

CONDITION	INTENSITY

FRUIT	FLOWER / HERB / OTHER

TASTING SHEET 12

PALATE / SMELL (CONTINUED)

AROMA	EARTH
OAK	OTHER / NOTES

STRUCTURE / TASTE

SWEETNESS	BODY
ACIDITY	ALCOHOL
TANNIN	COMPLEXITY
LENGTH	BALANCE

NOTES

DISCUSSION

NOTES	SUGGESTED PAIRINGS

SCORECARD

OVERALL QUALITY

1	2	3	4	5	6	7	8	9	10

TASTE

1	2	3	4	5	6	7	8	9	10

VALUE FOR MONEY

1	2	3	4	5	6	7	8	9	10

TASTING SHEET 13

WINE DETAILS

WINE NAME		DATE
PRODUCER		REGION / APPELLATION
VARIETAL		TYPE
VINTAGE	AGE	ALCOHOL %
PRICE	PURCHASED FROM	BOTTLE SIZE
NOTES		

VISUAL

CLARITY	BRIGHTNESS
INTENSITY	VISCOSITY
COLOR	SECONDARY COLOR
MENISCUS	OTHER / NOTES

PALATE / SMELL

CONDITION	INTENSITY
FRUIT	FLOWER / HERB / OTHER

TASTING SHEET 13

PALATE / SMELL (CONTINUED)

AROMA	EARTH
OAK	OTHER / NOTES

STRUCTURE / TASTE

SWEETNESS	BODY
ACIDITY	ALCOHOL
TANNIN	COMPLEXITY
LENGTH	BALANCE

NOTES	

DISCUSSION

NOTES	SUGGESTED PAIRINGS

SCORECARD

OVERALL QUALITY

1	2	3	4	5	6	7	8	9	10

TASTE

1	2	3	4	5	6	7	8	9	10

VALUE FOR MONEY

1	2	3	4	5	6	7	8	9	10

TASTING SHEET 14

WINE DETAILS

WINE NAME		DATE

PRODUCER	REGION / APPELLATION

VARIETAL	TYPE

VINTAGE	AGE	ALCOHOL %

PRICE	PURCHASED FROM	BOTTLE SIZE

NOTES

VISUAL

CLARITY	BRIGHTNESS

INTENSITY	VISCOSITY

COLOR	SECONDARY COLOR

MENISCUS	OTHER / NOTES

PALATE / SMELL

CONDITION	INTENSITY

FRUIT	FLOWER / HERB / OTHER

TASTING SHEET 14

PALATE / SMELL (CONTINUED)

AROMA	EARTH
OAK	OTHER / NOTES

STRUCTURE / TASTE

SWEETNESS	BODY
ACIDITY	ALCOHOL
TANNIN	COMPLEXITY
LENGTH	BALANCE

NOTES

DISCUSSION

NOTES	SUGGESTED PAIRINGS

SCORECARD

OVERALL QUALITY

1	2	3	4	5	6	7	8	9	10

TASTE

1	2	3	4	5	6	7	8	9	10

VALUE FOR MONEY

1	2	3	4	5	6	7	8	9	10

TASTING SHEET 15

WINE DETAILS

WINE NAME		DATE
PRODUCER		REGION / APPELLATION
VARIETAL		TYPE
VINTAGE	AGE	ALCOHOL %
PRICE	PURCHASED FROM	BOTTLE SIZE
NOTES		

VISUAL

CLARITY	BRIGHTNESS
INTENSITY	VISCOSITY
COLOR	SECONDARY COLOR
MENISCUS	OTHER / NOTES

PALATE / SMELL

CONDITION	INTENSITY
FRUIT	FLOWER / HERB / OTHER

TASTING SHEET 15

PALATE / SMELL (CONTINUED)

AROMA	EARTH
OAK	OTHER / NOTES

STRUCTURE / TASTE

SWEETNESS	BODY
ACIDITY	ALCOHOL
TANNIN	COMPLEXITY
LENGTH	BALANCE

NOTES

DISCUSSION

NOTES	SUGGESTED PAIRINGS

SCORECARD

OVERALL QUALITY

1	2	3	4	5	6	7	8	9	10

TASTE

1	2	3	4	5	6	7	8	9	10

VALUE FOR MONEY

1	2	3	4	5	6	7	8	9	10

TASTING SHEET 16

WINE DETAILS	
WINE NAME	DATE
PRODUCER	REGION / APPELLATION
VARIETAL	TYPE
VINTAGE / AGE	ALCOHOL %
PRICE / PURCHASED FROM	BOTTLE SIZE
NOTES	

VISUAL	
CLARITY	BRIGHTNESS
INTENSITY	VISCOSITY
COLOR	SECONDARY COLOR
MENISCUS	OTHER / NOTES

PALATE / SMELL	
CONDITION	INTENSITY
FRUIT	FLOWER / HERB / OTHER

TASTING SHEET 16

PALATE / SMELL (CONTINUED)

AROMA	EARTH
OAK	OTHER / NOTES

STRUCTURE / TASTE

SWEETNESS	BODY
ACIDITY	ALCOHOL
TANNIN	COMPLEXITY
LENGTH	BALANCE

NOTES

DISCUSSION

NOTES	SUGGESTED PAIRINGS

SCORECARD

OVERALL QUALITY

| 1 | 2 | 3 | 4 | 5 | 6 | 7 | 8 | 9 | 10 |

TASTE

| 1 | 2 | 3 | 4 | 5 | 6 | 7 | 8 | 9 | 10 |

VALUE FOR MONEY

| 1 | 2 | 3 | 4 | 5 | 6 | 7 | 8 | 9 | 10 |

TASTING SHEET 17

WINE DETAILS	
WINE NAME	DATE
PRODUCER	REGION / APPELLATION
VARIETAL	TYPE
VINTAGE	AGE	ALCOHOL %
PRICE	PURCHASED FROM	BOTTLE SIZE
NOTES	

VISUAL	
CLARITY	BRIGHTNESS
INTENSITY	VISCOSITY
COLOR	SECONDARY COLOR
MENISCUS	OTHER / NOTES

PALATE / SMELL	
CONDITION	INTENSITY
FRUIT	FLOWER / HERB / OTHER

TASTING SHEET 17

PALATE / SMELL (CONTINUED)

AROMA	EARTH
OAK	OTHER / NOTES

STRUCTURE / TASTE

SWEETNESS	BODY
ACIDITY	ALCOHOL
TANNIN	COMPLEXITY
LENGTH	BALANCE

NOTES

DISCUSSION

NOTES	SUGGESTED PAIRINGS

SCORECARD

OVERALL QUALITY

1	2	3	4	5	6	7	8	9	10

TASTE

1	2	3	4	5	6	7	8	9	10

VALUE FOR MONEY

1	2	3	4	5	6	7	8	9	10

TASTING SHEET 18

WINE DETAILS

WINE NAME		DATE
PRODUCER		REGION / APPELLATION
VARIETAL		TYPE
VINTAGE	AGE	ALCOHOL %
PRICE	PURCHASED FROM	BOTTLE SIZE

NOTES

VISUAL

CLARITY	BRIGHTNESS
INTENSITY	VISCOSITY
COLOR	SECONDARY COLOR
MENISCUS	OTHER / NOTES

PALATE / SMELL

CONDITION	INTENSITY
FRUIT	FLOWER / HERB / OTHER

TASTING SHEET 18

PALATE / SMELL (CONTINUED)	
AROMA	EARTH
OAK	OTHER / NOTES

STRUCTURE / TASTE	
SWEETNESS	BODY
ACIDITY	ALCOHOL
TANNIN	COMPLEXITY
LENGTH	BALANCE
NOTES	

DISCUSSION	
NOTES	SUGGESTED PAIRINGS

SCORECARD

OVERALL QUALITY

1	2	3	4	5	6	7	8	9	10

TASTE

1	2	3	4	5	6	7	8	9	10

VALUE FOR MONEY

1	2	3	4	5	6	7	8	9	10

TASTING SHEET 19

WINE DETAILS	
WINE NAME	DATE
PRODUCER	REGION / APPELLATION
VARIETAL	TYPE
VINTAGE	AGE	ALCOHOL %
PRICE	PURCHASED FROM	BOTTLE SIZE
NOTES	

VISUAL	
CLARITY	BRIGHTNESS
INTENSITY	VISCOSITY
COLOR	SECONDARY COLOR
MENISCUS	OTHER / NOTES

PALATE / SMELL	
CONDITION	INTENSITY
FRUIT	FLOWER / HERB / OTHER

TASTING SHEET 19

PALATE / SMELL (CONTINUED)	
AROMA	EARTH
OAK	OTHER / NOTES

STRUCTURE / TASTE	
SWEETNESS	BODY
ACIDITY	ALCOHOL
TANNIN	COMPLEXITY
LENGTH	BALANCE
NOTES	

DISCUSSION	
NOTES	SUGGESTED PAIRINGS

SCORECARD

OVERALL QUALITY

1	2	3	4	5	6	7	8	9	10

TASTE

1	2	3	4	5	6	7	8	9	10

VALUE FOR MONEY

1	2	3	4	5	6	7	8	9	10

TASTING SHEET 20

WINE DETAILS	
WINE NAME	DATE
PRODUCER	REGION / APPELLATION
VARIETAL	TYPE
VINTAGE	AGE	ALCOHOL %
PRICE	PURCHASED FROM	BOTTLE SIZE
NOTES	

VISUAL	
CLARITY	BRIGHTNESS
INTENSITY	VISCOSITY
COLOR	SECONDARY COLOR
MENISCUS	OTHER / NOTES

PALATE / SMELL	
CONDITION	INTENSITY
FRUIT	FLOWER / HERB / OTHER

TASTING SHEET 20

PALATE / SMELL (CONTINUED)

AROMA	EARTH
OAK	OTHER / NOTES

STRUCTURE / TASTE

SWEETNESS	BODY
ACIDITY	ALCOHOL
TANNIN	COMPLEXITY
LENGTH	BALANCE

NOTES

DISCUSSION

NOTES	SUGGESTED PAIRINGS

SCORECARD

OVERALL QUALITY

1	2	3	4	5	6	7	8	9	10

TASTE

1	2	3	4	5	6	7	8	9	10

VALUE FOR MONEY

1	2	3	4	5	6	7	8	9	10

TASTING SHEET 21

WINE DETAILS	
WINE NAME	DATE
PRODUCER	REGION / APPELLATION
VARIETAL	TYPE
VINTAGE	AGE	ALCOHOL %
PRICE	PURCHASED FROM	BOTTLE SIZE
NOTES	

VISUAL	
CLARITY	BRIGHTNESS
INTENSITY	VISCOSITY
COLOR	SECONDARY COLOR
MENISCUS	OTHER / NOTES

PALATE / SMELL	
CONDITION	INTENSITY
FRUIT	FLOWER / HERB / OTHER

TASTING SHEET 21

PALATE / SMELL (CONTINUED)	
AROMA	EARTH
OAK	OTHER / NOTES

STRUCTURE / TASTE	
SWEETNESS	BODY
ACIDITY	ALCOHOL
TANNIN	COMPLEXITY
LENGTH	BALANCE
NOTES	

DISCUSSION	
NOTES	SUGGESTED PAIRINGS

SCORECARD

OVERALL QUALITY

1	2	3	4	5	6	7	8	9	10

TASTE

1	2	3	4	5	6	7	8	9	10

VALUE FOR MONEY

1	2	3	4	5	6	7	8	9	10

TASTING SHEET 22

WINE DETAILS	
WINE NAME	DATE
PRODUCER	REGION / APPELLATION
VARIETAL	TYPE
VINTAGE / AGE	ALCOHOL %
PRICE / PURCHASED FROM	BOTTLE SIZE
NOTES	

VISUAL	
CLARITY	BRIGHTNESS
INTENSITY	VISCOSITY
COLOR	SECONDARY COLOR
MENISCUS	OTHER / NOTES

PALATE / SMELL	
CONDITION	INTENSITY
FRUIT	FLOWER / HERB / OTHER

TASTING SHEET 22

PALATE / SMELL (CONTINUED)	
AROMA	EARTH
OAK	OTHER / NOTES

STRUCTURE / TASTE	
SWEETNESS	BODY
ACIDITY	ALCOHOL
TANNIN	COMPLEXITY
LENGTH	BALANCE
NOTES	

DISCUSSION	
NOTES	SUGGESTED PAIRINGS

SCORECARD

OVERALL QUALITY

| 1 | 2 | 3 | 4 | 5 | 6 | 7 | 8 | 9 | 10 |

TASTE

| 1 | 2 | 3 | 4 | 5 | 6 | 7 | 8 | 9 | 10 |

VALUE FOR MONEY

| 1 | 2 | 3 | 4 | 5 | 6 | 7 | 8 | 9 | 10 |

TASTING SHEET 23

WINE DETAILS	
WINE NAME	DATE
PRODUCER	REGION / APPELLATION
VARIETAL	TYPE
VINTAGE	AGE	ALCOHOL %
PRICE	PURCHASED FROM	BOTTLE SIZE
NOTES	

VISUAL	
CLARITY	BRIGHTNESS
INTENSITY	VISCOSITY
COLOR	SECONDARY COLOR
MENISCUS	OTHER / NOTES

PALATE / SMELL	
CONDITION	INTENSITY
FRUIT	FLOWER / HERB / OTHER

TASTING SHEET 23

PALATE / SMELL (CONTINUED)

AROMA	EARTH
OAK	OTHER / NOTES

STRUCTURE / TASTE

SWEETNESS	BODY
ACIDITY	ALCOHOL
TANNIN	COMPLEXITY
LENGTH	BALANCE

NOTES

DISCUSSION

NOTES	SUGGESTED PAIRINGS

SCORECARD

OVERALL QUALITY

1	2	3	4	5	6	7	8	9	10

TASTE

1	2	3	4	5	6	7	8	9	10

VALUE FOR MONEY

1	2	3	4	5	6	7	8	9	10

TASTING SHEET 24

WINE DETAILS	
WINE NAME	DATE
PRODUCER	REGION / APPELLATION
VARIETAL	TYPE
VINTAGE	AGE	ALCOHOL %
PRICE	PURCHASED FROM	BOTTLE SIZE
NOTES	

VISUAL	
CLARITY	BRIGHTNESS
INTENSITY	VISCOSITY
COLOR	SECONDARY COLOR
MENISCUS	OTHER / NOTES

PALATE / SMELL	
CONDITION	INTENSITY
FRUIT	FLOWER / HERB / OTHER

TASTING SHEET 24

PALATE / SMELL (CONTINUED)

AROMA	EARTH
OAK	OTHER / NOTES

STRUCTURE / TASTE

SWEETNESS	BODY
ACIDITY	ALCOHOL
TANNIN	COMPLEXITY
LENGTH	BALANCE
NOTES	

DISCUSSION

NOTES	SUGGESTED PAIRINGS

SCORECARD

OVERALL QUALITY
1	2	3	4	5	6	7	8	9	10

TASTE
1	2	3	4	5	6	7	8	9	10

VALUE FOR MONEY
1	2	3	4	5	6	7	8	9	10

TASTING SHEET 25

WINE DETAILS

WINE NAME		DATE
PRODUCER		REGION / APPELLATION
VARIETAL		TYPE
VINTAGE	AGE	ALCOHOL %
PRICE	PURCHASED FROM	BOTTLE SIZE
NOTES		

VISUAL

CLARITY	BRIGHTNESS
INTENSITY	VISCOSITY
COLOR	SECONDARY COLOR
MENISCUS	OTHER / NOTES

PALATE / SMELL

CONDITION	INTENSITY
FRUIT	FLOWER / HERB / OTHER

PALATE / SMELL (CONTINUED)

AROMA	EARTH
OAK	OTHER / NOTES

STRUCTURE / TASTE

SWEETNESS	BODY
ACIDITY	ALCOHOL
TANNIN	COMPLEXITY
LENGTH	BALANCE

NOTES

DISCUSSION

NOTES	SUGGESTED PAIRINGS

SCORECARD

OVERALL QUALITY

1	2	3	4	5	6	7	8	9	10

TASTE

1	2	3	4	5	6	7	8	9	10

VALUE FOR MONEY

1	2	3	4	5	6	7	8	9	10

TASTING SHEET **26**

WINE DETAILS

WINE NAME		DATE
PRODUCER		REGION / APPELLATION
VARIETAL		TYPE
VINTAGE	AGE	ALCOHOL %
PRICE	PURCHASED FROM	BOTTLE SIZE
NOTES		

VISUAL

CLARITY	BRIGHTNESS
INTENSITY	VISCOSITY
COLOR	SECONDARY COLOR
MENISCUS	OTHER / NOTES

PALATE / SMELL

CONDITION	INTENSITY
FRUIT	FLOWER / HERB / OTHER

TASTING SHEET 26

PALATE / SMELL (CONTINUED)	
AROMA	EARTH
OAK	OTHER / NOTES

STRUCTURE / TASTE	
SWEETNESS	BODY
ACIDITY	ALCOHOL
TANNIN	COMPLEXITY
LENGTH	BALANCE

NOTES

DISCUSSION	
NOTES	SUGGESTED PAIRINGS

SCORECARD

OVERALL QUALITY

1	2	3	4	5	6	7	8	9	10

TASTE

1	2	3	4	5	6	7	8	9	10

VALUE FOR MONEY

1	2	3	4	5	6	7	8	9	10

TASTING SHEET 27

WINE DETAILS	
WINE NAME	DATE
PRODUCER	REGION / APPELLATION
VARIETAL	TYPE
VINTAGE / AGE	ALCOHOL %
PRICE / PURCHASED FROM	BOTTLE SIZE
NOTES	

VISUAL	
CLARITY	BRIGHTNESS
INTENSITY	VISCOSITY
COLOR	SECONDARY COLOR
MENISCUS	OTHER / NOTES

PALATE / SMELL	
CONDITION	INTENSITY
FRUIT	FLOWER / HERB / OTHER

TASTING SHEET 27

PALATE / SMELL (CONTINUED)

AROMA	EARTH
OAK	OTHER / NOTES

STRUCTURE / TASTE

SWEETNESS	BODY
ACIDITY	ALCOHOL
TANNIN	COMPLEXITY
LENGTH	BALANCE
NOTES	

DISCUSSION

NOTES	SUGGESTED PAIRINGS

SCORECARD

OVERALL QUALITY

1	2	3	4	5	6	7	8	9	10

TASTE

1	2	3	4	5	6	7	8	9	10

VALUE FOR MONEY

1	2	3	4	5	6	7	8	9	10

TASTING SHEET 28

WINE DETAILS	
WINE NAME	DATE
PRODUCER	REGION / APPELLATION
VARIETAL	TYPE
VINTAGE / AGE	ALCOHOL %
PRICE / PURCHASED FROM	BOTTLE SIZE
NOTES	

VISUAL	
CLARITY	BRIGHTNESS
INTENSITY	VISCOSITY
COLOR	SECONDARY COLOR
MENISCUS	OTHER / NOTES

PALATE / SMELL	
CONDITION	INTENSITY
FRUIT	FLOWER / HERB / OTHER

TASTING SHEET 28

PALATE / SMELL (CONTINUED)

AROMA	EARTH
OAK	OTHER / NOTES

STRUCTURE / TASTE

SWEETNESS	BODY
ACIDITY	ALCOHOL
TANNIN	COMPLEXITY
LENGTH	BALANCE

NOTES

DISCUSSION

NOTES	SUGGESTED PAIRINGS

SCORECARD

OVERALL QUALITY

1	2	3	4	5	6	7	8	9	10

TASTE

1	2	3	4	5	6	7	8	9	10

VALUE FOR MONEY

1	2	3	4	5	6	7	8	9	10

TASTING SHEET 29

WINE DETAILS			
WINE NAME			DATE
PRODUCER			REGION / APPELLATION
VARIETAL			TYPE
VINTAGE	AGE		ALCOHOL %
PRICE	PURCHASED FROM		BOTTLE SIZE
NOTES			

VISUAL	
CLARITY	BRIGHTNESS
INTENSITY	VISCOSITY
COLOR	SECONDARY COLOR
MENISCUS	OTHER / NOTES

PALATE / SMELL	
CONDITION	INTENSITY
FRUIT	FLOWER / HERB / OTHER

TASTING SHEET 29

PALATE / SMELL (CONTINUED)

AROMA	EARTH
OAK	OTHER / NOTES

STRUCTURE / TASTE

SWEETNESS	BODY
ACIDITY	ALCOHOL
TANNIN	COMPLEXITY
LENGTH	BALANCE

NOTES

DISCUSSION

NOTES	SUGGESTED PAIRINGS

SCORECARD

OVERALL QUALITY

1	2	3	4	5	6	7	8	9	10

TASTE

1	2	3	4	5	6	7	8	9	10

VALUE FOR MONEY

1	2	3	4	5	6	7	8	9	10

TASTING SHEET 30

WINE DETAILS

WINE NAME		DATE
PRODUCER		REGION / APPELLATION
VARIETAL		TYPE

VINTAGE	AGE	ALCOHOL %
PRICE	PURCHASED FROM	BOTTLE SIZE

NOTES

VISUAL

CLARITY	BRIGHTNESS
INTENSITY	VISCOSITY
COLOR	SECONDARY COLOR
MENISCUS	OTHER / NOTES

PALATE / SMELL

CONDITION	INTENSITY
FRUIT	FLOWER / HERB / OTHER

TASTING SHEET 30

PALATE / SMELL (CONTINUED)	
AROMA	EARTH
OAK	OTHER / NOTES

STRUCTURE / TASTE	
SWEETNESS	BODY
ACIDITY	ALCOHOL
TANNIN	COMPLEXITY
LENGTH	BALANCE
NOTES	

DISCUSSION	
NOTES	SUGGESTED PAIRINGS

SCORECARD

OVERALL QUALITY

| 1 | 2 | 3 | 4 | 5 | 6 | 7 | 8 | 9 | 10 |

TASTE

| 1 | 2 | 3 | 4 | 5 | 6 | 7 | 8 | 9 | 10 |

VALUE FOR MONEY

| 1 | 2 | 3 | 4 | 5 | 6 | 7 | 8 | 9 | 10 |

TASTING SHEET 31

WINE DETAILS	
WINE NAME	DATE
PRODUCER	REGION / APPELLATION
VARIETAL	TYPE
VINTAGE	AGE	ALCOHOL %
PRICE	PURCHASED FROM	BOTTLE SIZE
NOTES	

VISUAL	
CLARITY	BRIGHTNESS
INTENSITY	VISCOSITY
COLOR	SECONDARY COLOR
MENISCUS	OTHER / NOTES

PALATE / SMELL	
CONDITION	INTENSITY
FRUIT	FLOWER / HERB / OTHER

TASTING SHEET 31

PALATE / SMELL (CONTINUED)

AROMA	EARTH
OAK	OTHER / NOTES

STRUCTURE / TASTE

SWEETNESS	BODY
ACIDITY	ALCOHOL
TANNIN	COMPLEXITY
LENGTH	BALANCE

NOTES

DISCUSSION

NOTES	SUGGESTED PAIRINGS

SCORECARD

OVERALL QUALITY

1	2	3	4	5	6	7	8	9	10

TASTE

1	2	3	4	5	6	7	8	9	10

VALUE FOR MONEY

1	2	3	4	5	6	7	8	9	10

TASTING SHEET 32

WINE DETAILS	
WINE NAME	DATE
PRODUCER	REGION / APPELLATION
VARIETAL	TYPE
VINTAGE	AGE	ALCOHOL %
PRICE	PURCHASED FROM	BOTTLE SIZE
NOTES	

VISUAL	
CLARITY	BRIGHTNESS
INTENSITY	VISCOSITY
COLOR	SECONDARY COLOR
MENISCUS	OTHER / NOTES

PALATE / SMELL	
CONDITION	INTENSITY
FRUIT	FLOWER / HERB / OTHER

TASTING SHEET 32

PALATE / SMELL (CONTINUED)	
AROMA	EARTH
OAK	OTHER / NOTES

STRUCTURE / TASTE	
SWEETNESS	BODY
ACIDITY	ALCOHOL
TANNIN	COMPLEXITY
LENGTH	BALANCE

NOTES

DISCUSSION	
NOTES	SUGGESTED PAIRINGS

SCORECARD

OVERALL QUALITY

1	2	3	4	5	6	7	8	9	10

TASTE

1	2	3	4	5	6	7	8	9	10

VALUE FOR MONEY

1	2	3	4	5	6	7	8	9	10

TASTING SHEET 33

WINE DETAILS	
WINE NAME	DATE
PRODUCER	REGION / APPELLATION
VARIETAL	TYPE
VINTAGE	AGE	ALCOHOL %
PRICE	PURCHASED FROM	BOTTLE SIZE
NOTES	

VISUAL	
CLARITY	BRIGHTNESS
INTENSITY	VISCOSITY
COLOR	SECONDARY COLOR
MENISCUS	OTHER / NOTES

PALATE / SMELL	
CONDITION	INTENSITY
FRUIT	FLOWER / HERB / OTHER

TASTING SHEET 33

PALATE / SMELL (CONTINUED)	
AROMA	EARTH
OAK	OTHER / NOTES

STRUCTURE / TASTE	
SWEETNESS	BODY
ACIDITY	ALCOHOL
TANNIN	COMPLEXITY
LENGTH	BALANCE
NOTES	

DISCUSSION	
NOTES	SUGGESTED PAIRINGS

SCORECARD

OVERALL QUALITY

1	2	3	4	5	6	7	8	9	10

TASTE

1	2	3	4	5	6	7	8	9	10

VALUE FOR MONEY

1	2	3	4	5	6	7	8	9	10

TASTING SHEET 34

WINE DETAILS	
WINE NAME	DATE
PRODUCER	REGION / APPELLATION
VARIETAL	TYPE
VINTAGE	AGE	ALCOHOL %
PRICE	PURCHASED FROM	BOTTLE SIZE
NOTES	

VISUAL	
CLARITY	BRIGHTNESS
INTENSITY	VISCOSITY
COLOR	SECONDARY COLOR
MENISCUS	OTHER / NOTES

PALATE / SMELL	
CONDITION	INTENSITY
FRUIT	FLOWER / HERB / OTHER

TASTING SHEET 34

PALATE / SMELL (CONTINUED)

AROMA	EARTH
OAK	OTHER / NOTES

STRUCTURE / TASTE

SWEETNESS	BODY
ACIDITY	ALCOHOL
TANNIN	COMPLEXITY
LENGTH	BALANCE

NOTES

DISCUSSION

NOTES	SUGGESTED PAIRINGS

SCORECARD

OVERALL QUALITY

1	2	3	4	5	6	7	8	9	10

TASTE

1	2	3	4	5	6	7	8	9	10

VALUE FOR MONEY

1	2	3	4	5	6	7	8	9	10

TASTING SHEET 35

WINE DETAILS	
WINE NAME	DATE
PRODUCER	REGION / APPELLATION
VARIETAL	TYPE
VINTAGE	AGE	ALCOHOL %
PRICE	PURCHASED FROM	BOTTLE SIZE
NOTES	

VISUAL	
CLARITY	BRIGHTNESS
INTENSITY	VISCOSITY
COLOR	SECONDARY COLOR
MENISCUS	OTHER / NOTES

PALATE / SMELL	
CONDITION	INTENSITY
FRUIT	FLOWER / HERB / OTHER

TASTING SHEET 35

PALATE / SMELL (CONTINUED)

AROMA	EARTH
OAK	OTHER / NOTES

STRUCTURE / TASTE

SWEETNESS	BODY
ACIDITY	ALCOHOL
TANNIN	COMPLEXITY
LENGTH	BALANCE

NOTES

DISCUSSION

NOTES	SUGGESTED PAIRINGS

SCORECARD

OVERALL QUALITY

1	2	3	4	5	6	7	8	9	10

TASTE

1	2	3	4	5	6	7	8	9	10

VALUE FOR MONEY

1	2	3	4	5	6	7	8	9	10

TASTING SHEET 36

WINE DETAILS	
WINE NAME	DATE
PRODUCER	REGION / APPELLATION
VARIETAL	TYPE
VINTAGE	AGE	ALCOHOL %
PRICE	PURCHASED FROM	BOTTLE SIZE
NOTES	

VISUAL	
CLARITY	BRIGHTNESS
INTENSITY	VISCOSITY
COLOR	SECONDARY COLOR
MENISCUS	OTHER / NOTES

PALATE / SMELL	
CONDITION	INTENSITY
FRUIT	FLOWER / HERB / OTHER

TASTING SHEET 36

PALATE / SMELL (CONTINUED)	
AROMA	EARTH
OAK	OTHER / NOTES

STRUCTURE / TASTE	
SWEETNESS	BODY
ACIDITY	ALCOHOL
TANNIN	COMPLEXITY
LENGTH	BALANCE
NOTES	

DISCUSSION	
NOTES	SUGGESTED PAIRINGS

SCORECARD

OVERALL QUALITY

1	2	3	4	5	6	7	8	9	10

TASTE

1	2	3	4	5	6	7	8	9	10

VALUE FOR MONEY

1	2	3	4	5	6	7	8	9	10

TASTING SHEET 37

WINE DETAILS	
WINE NAME	DATE
PRODUCER	REGION / APPELLATION
VARIETAL	TYPE

VINTAGE	AGE	ALCOHOL %
PRICE	PURCHASED FROM	BOTTLE SIZE

NOTES

VISUAL	
CLARITY	BRIGHTNESS
INTENSITY	VISCOSITY
COLOR	SECONDARY COLOR
MENISCUS	OTHER / NOTES
PALATE / SMELL	
CONDITION	INTENSITY
FRUIT	FLOWER / HERB / OTHER

TASTING SHEET 37

PALATE / SMELL (CONTINUED)

AROMA	EARTH
OAK	OTHER / NOTES

STRUCTURE / TASTE

SWEETNESS	BODY
ACIDITY	ALCOHOL
TANNIN	COMPLEXITY
LENGTH	BALANCE

NOTES

DISCUSSION

NOTES	SUGGESTED PAIRINGS

SCORECARD

OVERALL QUALITY

| 1 | 2 | 3 | 4 | 5 | 6 | 7 | 8 | 9 | 10 |

TASTE

| 1 | 2 | 3 | 4 | 5 | 6 | 7 | 8 | 9 | 10 |

VALUE FOR MONEY

| 1 | 2 | 3 | 4 | 5 | 6 | 7 | 8 | 9 | 10 |

TASTING SHEET 38

WINE DETAILS	
WINE NAME	DATE
PRODUCER	REGION / APPELLATION
VARIETAL	TYPE
VINTAGE	AGE	ALCOHOL %
PRICE	PURCHASED FROM	BOTTLE SIZE
NOTES	

VISUAL	
CLARITY	BRIGHTNESS
INTENSITY	VISCOSITY
COLOR	SECONDARY COLOR
MENISCUS	OTHER / NOTES

PALATE / SMELL	
CONDITION	INTENSITY
FRUIT	FLOWER / HERB / OTHER

TASTING SHEET 38

PALATE / SMELL (CONTINUED)

AROMA	EARTH
OAK	OTHER / NOTES

STRUCTURE / TASTE

SWEETNESS	BODY
ACIDITY	ALCOHOL
TANNIN	COMPLEXITY
LENGTH	BALANCE

NOTES

DISCUSSION

NOTES	SUGGESTED PAIRINGS

SCORECARD

OVERALL QUALITY

1	2	3	4	5	6	7	8	9	10

TASTE

1	2	3	4	5	6	7	8	9	10

VALUE FOR MONEY

1	2	3	4	5	6	7	8	9	10

TASTING SHEET 39

WINE DETAILS	
WINE NAME	DATE
PRODUCER	REGION / APPELLATION
VARIETAL	TYPE
VINTAGE	AGE	ALCOHOL %
PRICE	PURCHASED FROM	BOTTLE SIZE
NOTES	

VISUAL	
CLARITY	BRIGHTNESS
INTENSITY	VISCOSITY
COLOR	SECONDARY COLOR
MENISCUS	OTHER / NOTES

PALATE / SMELL	
CONDITION	INTENSITY
FRUIT	FLOWER / HERB / OTHER

TASTING SHEET 39

PALATE / SMELL (CONTINUED)

AROMA	EARTH
OAK	OTHER / NOTES

STRUCTURE / TASTE

SWEETNESS	BODY
ACIDITY	ALCOHOL
TANNIN	COMPLEXITY
LENGTH	BALANCE

NOTES

DISCUSSION

NOTES	SUGGESTED PAIRINGS

SCORECARD

OVERALL QUALITY

1	2	3	4	5	6	7	8	9	10

TASTE

1	2	3	4	5	6	7	8	9	10

VALUE FOR MONEY

1	2	3	4	5	6	7	8	9	10

TASTING SHEET 40

WINE DETAILS			
WINE NAME			DATE
PRODUCER			REGION / APPELLATION
VARIETAL			TYPE
VINTAGE	AGE		ALCOHOL %
PRICE	PURCHASED FROM		BOTTLE SIZE
NOTES			

VISUAL	
CLARITY	BRIGHTNESS
INTENSITY	VISCOSITY
COLOR	SECONDARY COLOR
MENISCUS	OTHER / NOTES

PALATE / SMELL	
CONDITION	INTENSITY
FRUIT	FLOWER / HERB / OTHER

TASTING SHEET 40

PALATE / SMELL (CONTINUED)

AROMA	EARTH
OAK	OTHER / NOTES

STRUCTURE / TASTE

SWEETNESS	BODY
ACIDITY	ALCOHOL
TANNIN	COMPLEXITY
LENGTH	BALANCE

NOTES

DISCUSSION

NOTES	SUGGESTED PAIRINGS

SCORECARD

OVERALL QUALITY

1	2	3	4	5	6	7	8	9	10

TASTE

1	2	3	4	5	6	7	8	9	10

VALUE FOR MONEY

1	2	3	4	5	6	7	8	9	10

TASTING SHEET 41

WINE DETAILS	
WINE NAME	DATE
PRODUCER	REGION / APPELLATION
VARIETAL	TYPE
VINTAGE	AGE	ALCOHOL %
PRICE	PURCHASED FROM	BOTTLE SIZE
NOTES	

VISUAL	
CLARITY	BRIGHTNESS
INTENSITY	VISCOSITY
COLOR	SECONDARY COLOR
MENISCUS	OTHER / NOTES

PALATE / SMELL	
CONDITION	INTENSITY
FRUIT	FLOWER / HERB / OTHER

TASTING SHEET 41

PALATE / SMELL (CONTINUED)

AROMA	EARTH
OAK	OTHER / NOTES

STRUCTURE / TASTE

SWEETNESS	BODY
ACIDITY	ALCOHOL
TANNIN	COMPLEXITY
LENGTH	BALANCE

NOTES

DISCUSSION

NOTES	SUGGESTED PAIRINGS

SCORECARD

OVERALL QUALITY

| 1 | 2 | 3 | 4 | 5 | 6 | 7 | 8 | 9 | 10 |

TASTE

| 1 | 2 | 3 | 4 | 5 | 6 | 7 | 8 | 9 | 10 |

VALUE FOR MONEY

| 1 | 2 | 3 | 4 | 5 | 6 | 7 | 8 | 9 | 10 |

TASTING SHEET 42

WINE DETAILS	
WINE NAME	DATE
PRODUCER	REGION / APPELLATION
VARIETAL	TYPE
VINTAGE	AGE	ALCOHOL %
PRICE	PURCHASED FROM	BOTTLE SIZE
NOTES	

VISUAL	
CLARITY	BRIGHTNESS
INTENSITY	VISCOSITY
COLOR	SECONDARY COLOR
MENISCUS	OTHER / NOTES

PALATE / SMELL	
CONDITION	INTENSITY
FRUIT	FLOWER / HERB / OTHER

TASTING SHEET 42

PALATE / SMELL (CONTINUED)

AROMA	EARTH
OAK	OTHER / NOTES

STRUCTURE / TASTE

SWEETNESS	BODY
ACIDITY	ALCOHOL
TANNIN	COMPLEXITY
LENGTH	BALANCE

NOTES

DISCUSSION

NOTES	SUGGESTED PAIRINGS

SCORECARD

OVERALL QUALITY

1	2	3	4	5	6	7	8	9	10

TASTE

1	2	3	4	5	6	7	8	9	10

VALUE FOR MONEY

1	2	3	4	5	6	7	8	9	10

TASTING SHEET 43

WINE DETAILS	
WINE NAME	DATE
PRODUCER	REGION / APPELLATION
VARIETAL	TYPE
VINTAGE	AGE	ALCOHOL %
PRICE	PURCHASED FROM	BOTTLE SIZE
NOTES	

VISUAL	
CLARITY	BRIGHTNESS
INTENSITY	VISCOSITY
COLOR	SECONDARY COLOR
MENISCUS	OTHER / NOTES

PALATE / SMELL	
CONDITION	INTENSITY
FRUIT	FLOWER / HERB / OTHER

TASTING SHEET 43

PALATE / SMELL (CONTINUED)

AROMA	EARTH
OAK	OTHER / NOTES

STRUCTURE / TASTE

SWEETNESS	BODY
ACIDITY	ALCOHOL
TANNIN	COMPLEXITY
LENGTH	BALANCE

NOTES

DISCUSSION

NOTES	SUGGESTED PAIRINGS

SCORECARD

OVERALL QUALITY

| 1 | 2 | 3 | 4 | 5 | 6 | 7 | 8 | 9 | 10 |

TASTE

| 1 | 2 | 3 | 4 | 5 | 6 | 7 | 8 | 9 | 10 |

VALUE FOR MONEY

| 1 | 2 | 3 | 4 | 5 | 6 | 7 | 8 | 9 | 10 |

TASTING SHEET 44

WINE DETAILS

WINE NAME		DATE
PRODUCER		REGION / APPELLATION
VARIETAL		TYPE
VINTAGE	AGE	ALCOHOL %
PRICE	PURCHASED FROM	BOTTLE SIZE

NOTES

VISUAL

CLARITY	BRIGHTNESS
INTENSITY	VISCOSITY
COLOR	SECONDARY COLOR
MENISCUS	OTHER / NOTES

PALATE / SMELL

CONDITION	INTENSITY
FRUIT	FLOWER / HERB / OTHER

TASTING SHEET 44

PALATE / SMELL (CONTINUED)

AROMA	EARTH
OAK	OTHER / NOTES

STRUCTURE / TASTE

SWEETNESS	BODY
ACIDITY	ALCOHOL
TANNIN	COMPLEXITY
LENGTH	BALANCE

NOTES

DISCUSSION

NOTES	SUGGESTED PAIRINGS

SCORECARD

OVERALL QUALITY

1	2	3	4	5	6	7	8	9	10

TASTE

1	2	3	4	5	6	7	8	9	10

VALUE FOR MONEY

1	2	3	4	5	6	7	8	9	10

TASTING SHEET 45

WINE DETAILS	
WINE NAME	DATE
PRODUCER	REGION / APPELLATION
VARIETAL	TYPE
VINTAGE	AGE	ALCOHOL %
PRICE	PURCHASED FROM	BOTTLE SIZE
NOTES	

VISUAL	
CLARITY	BRIGHTNESS
INTENSITY	VISCOSITY
COLOR	SECONDARY COLOR
MENISCUS	OTHER / NOTES

PALATE / SMELL	
CONDITION	INTENSITY
FRUIT	FLOWER / HERB / OTHER

TASTING SHEET 45

PALATE / SMELL (CONTINUED)

AROMA	EARTH
OAK	OTHER / NOTES

STRUCTURE / TASTE

SWEETNESS	BODY
ACIDITY	ALCOHOL
TANNIN	COMPLEXITY
LENGTH	BALANCE

NOTES

DISCUSSION

NOTES	SUGGESTED PAIRINGS

SCORECARD

OVERALL QUALITY

| 1 | 2 | 3 | 4 | 5 | 6 | 7 | 8 | 9 | 10 |

TASTE

| 1 | 2 | 3 | 4 | 5 | 6 | 7 | 8 | 9 | 10 |

VALUE FOR MONEY

| 1 | 2 | 3 | 4 | 5 | 6 | 7 | 8 | 9 | 10 |

TASTING SHEET 46

WINE DETAILS	
WINE NAME	DATE
PRODUCER	REGION / APPELLATION
VARIETAL	TYPE
VINTAGE	AGE	ALCOHOL %
PRICE	PURCHASED FROM	BOTTLE SIZE
NOTES	

VISUAL	
CLARITY	BRIGHTNESS
INTENSITY	VISCOSITY
COLOR	SECONDARY COLOR
MENISCUS	OTHER / NOTES

PALATE / SMELL	
CONDITION	INTENSITY
FRUIT	FLOWER / HERB / OTHER

TASTING SHEET 46

PALATE / SMELL (CONTINUED)

AROMA	EARTH
OAK	OTHER / NOTES

STRUCTURE / TASTE

SWEETNESS	BODY
ACIDITY	ALCOHOL
TANNIN	COMPLEXITY
LENGTH	BALANCE

NOTES

DISCUSSION

NOTES	SUGGESTED PAIRINGS

SCORECARD

OVERALL QUALITY

1	2	3	4	5	6	7	8	9	10

TASTE

1	2	3	4	5	6	7	8	9	10

VALUE FOR MONEY

1	2	3	4	5	6	7	8	9	10

TASTING SHEET 47

WINE DETAILS	
WINE NAME	DATE
PRODUCER	REGION / APPELLATION
VARIETAL	TYPE
VINTAGE	AGE	ALCOHOL %
PRICE	PURCHASED FROM	BOTTLE SIZE
NOTES	

VISUAL	
CLARITY	BRIGHTNESS
INTENSITY	VISCOSITY
COLOR	SECONDARY COLOR
MENISCUS	OTHER / NOTES

PALATE / SMELL	
CONDITION	INTENSITY
FRUIT	FLOWER / HERB / OTHER

TASTING SHEET 47

PALATE / SMELL (CONTINUED)	
AROMA	EARTH
OAK	OTHER / NOTES

STRUCTURE / TASTE	
SWEETNESS	BODY
ACIDITY	ALCOHOL
TANNIN	COMPLEXITY
LENGTH	BALANCE
NOTES	

DISCUSSION	
NOTES	SUGGESTED PAIRINGS

SCORECARD

OVERALL QUALITY

| 1 | 2 | 3 | 4 | 5 | 6 | 7 | 8 | 9 | 10 |

TASTE

| 1 | 2 | 3 | 4 | 5 | 6 | 7 | 8 | 9 | 10 |

VALUE FOR MONEY

| 1 | 2 | 3 | 4 | 5 | 6 | 7 | 8 | 9 | 10 |

TASTING SHEET 48

WINE DETAILS	
WINE NAME	DATE
PRODUCER	REGION / APPELLATION
VARIETAL	TYPE

VINTAGE	AGE	ALCOHOL %
PRICE	PURCHASED FROM	BOTTLE SIZE

NOTES

VISUAL	
CLARITY	BRIGHTNESS
INTENSITY	VISCOSITY
COLOR	SECONDARY COLOR
MENISCUS	OTHER / NOTES

PALATE / SMELL	
CONDITION	INTENSITY
FRUIT	FLOWER / HERB / OTHER

TASTING SHEET 48

PALATE / SMELL (CONTINUED)	
AROMA	EARTH
OAK	OTHER / NOTES

STRUCTURE / TASTE	
SWEETNESS	BODY
ACIDITY	ALCOHOL
TANNIN	COMPLEXITY
LENGTH	BALANCE
NOTES	

DISCUSSION	
NOTES	SUGGESTED PAIRINGS

SCORECARD

OVERALL QUALITY

1	2	3	4	5	6	7	8	9	10

TASTE

1	2	3	4	5	6	7	8	9	10

VALUE FOR MONEY

1	2	3	4	5	6	7	8	9	10

TASTING SHEET 49

WINE DETAILS	
WINE NAME	DATE
PRODUCER	REGION / APPELLATION
VARIETAL	TYPE
VINTAGE	AGE	ALCOHOL %
PRICE	PURCHASED FROM	BOTTLE SIZE
NOTES	

VISUAL	
CLARITY	BRIGHTNESS
INTENSITY	VISCOSITY
COLOR	SECONDARY COLOR
MENISCUS	OTHER / NOTES

PALATE / SMELL	
CONDITION	INTENSITY
FRUIT	FLOWER / HERB / OTHER

TASTING SHEET 49

PALATE / SMELL (CONTINUED)

AROMA	EARTH
OAK	OTHER / NOTES

STRUCTURE / TASTE

SWEETNESS	BODY
ACIDITY	ALCOHOL
TANNIN	COMPLEXITY
LENGTH	BALANCE

NOTES

DISCUSSION

NOTES	SUGGESTED PAIRINGS

SCORECARD

OVERALL QUALITY

| 1 | 2 | 3 | 4 | 5 | 6 | 7 | 8 | 9 | 10 |

TASTE

| 1 | 2 | 3 | 4 | 5 | 6 | 7 | 8 | 9 | 10 |

VALUE FOR MONEY

| 1 | 2 | 3 | 4 | 5 | 6 | 7 | 8 | 9 | 10 |

TASTING SHEET 50

WINE DETAILS	
WINE NAME	DATE
PRODUCER	REGION / APPELLATION
VARIETAL	TYPE
VINTAGE	AGE	ALCOHOL %
PRICE	PURCHASED FROM	BOTTLE SIZE
NOTES	

VISUAL	
CLARITY	BRIGHTNESS
INTENSITY	VISCOSITY
COLOR	SECONDARY COLOR
MENISCUS	OTHER / NOTES

PALATE / SMELL	
CONDITION	INTENSITY
FRUIT	FLOWER / HERB / OTHER

TASTING SHEET 50

PALATE / SMELL (CONTINUED)

AROMA	EARTH
OAK	OTHER / NOTES

STRUCTURE / TASTE

SWEETNESS	BODY
ACIDITY	ALCOHOL
TANNIN	COMPLEXITY
LENGTH	BALANCE

NOTES

DISCUSSION

NOTES	SUGGESTED PAIRINGS

SCORECARD

OVERALL QUALITY

1	2	3	4	5	6	7	8	9	10

TASTE

1	2	3	4	5	6	7	8	9	10

VALUE FOR MONEY

1	2	3	4	5	6	7	8	9	10

NOTES

NOTES

NOTES

NOTES

NOTES

NOTES

NOTES

NOTES

NOTES

NOTES

NOTES

NOTES

NOTES

NOTES

GLOSSARY

TERMINOLOGY

Varietal: Type of Grape

Type: Red, white, bubbly, chardonnay etc

Vintage: Year in which grapes were picked

Viscosity: Liquid consistency (Watery, Thick)

Meniscus: Attraction of particles to glass or each other

Tannin: Bitterness / Astringent

Length: How long the flavors of a wine last on your palate after wine has been swallowed or spit

Below are some words you may wish to use when describing the wine. Note that you may choose to use your own descriptive words.

VISUAL

Clarity: Clear, Slight Haze, Murky, Sediment, Gassy / Bubbly

Brightness: Dull, Day bright, Slight Brightness, Brilliant

Intensity: Low, Medium, High, Extreme

Viscosity: Low, Medium, High, Extreme, Watery, Thick

Color:

    Red: Garnet, Ruby, Purple

    White: Snow, Yellow, Gold

Secondary Color:

    Red: Red base, Blue Base

    White: Green, Copper, Amber

Meniscus: Yes / No, width, color variation, clarity, shape (concave)

GLOSSARY

PALATE / SMELL

Condition: Sound / Unsound, Clean / Faulty

Intensity: Low, Medium, High, Extreme

Aroma: Youthful, aged, Slight

Fruit: Class of fruits (Citrus, red fruits, dark fruits etc). Fruit flavors, style (Dried, fresh etc)

Flower / Herb: Flowers, herbs, vegetables, oxidation, lees, botrytis, MLF

Earth: Yes / No, organic earth, inorganic

Oak: Yes / No, European / American, new / neutral

STRUCTURE / TASTE

Sweetness: Dry, Off-Dry, Semi-Sweet, Medium, Sweet

Body: Low, Medium, High, Extreme

Acidity: Low, Medium, High, Extreme

Alcohol: Low, Medium, High, Extreme

Tannin: Low, Medium, High, Extreme

Complexity: Low, Medium, High, Extreme

Length: Low, Medium, Long, Extreme

Balance: In / out balance

THANK-YOU!

We hope you enjoyed your wine tasting journey

Please consider leaving an honest review on **Amazon** if you get the chance. We really appreciate every comment and review!